Kilimanjaro via the
Marangu Route

Kilimanjaro via the Marangu Route

✦

"Tourist Route" My Ass

Phil Gray

iUniverse, Inc.
New York Lincoln Shanghai

Kilimanjaro via the Marangu Route
"Tourist Route" My Ass

iUniverse books may be ordered through booksellers or by contacting:

iUniverse
2021 Pine Lake Road, Suite 100
Lincoln, NE 68512
www.iuniverse.com
1-800-Authors (1-800-288-4677)

ISBN-13: 978-0-595-41625-7 (pbk)
ISBN-13: 978-0-595-85973-3 (ebk)
ISBN-10: 0-595-41625-X (pbk)
ISBN-10: 0-595-85973-9 (ebk)

Printed in the United States of America

Melinda, thanks for the inspiration.

Contents

Background

1996 WAS NOT a good year. My business life was so bad I felt like I had the reverse-Midas touch. Everything I touched turned to shit. And no amount of good old-fashioned hard work made a lick of difference. Nothing worked and my frustration mounted. So I decided to disengage; to clear the slate completely with an off-the-wall dalliance of the kind an analyst would discourage and my wife would forbid. An all-boys' adventure in a faraway land. An adventure far away from telephones and faxes and lawyers. An adventure with an abundance of humor, serious physical exertion, and danger nominally short of life-threatening.

Bingo!

For years, I had been vaguely aware that there are some small hotels located on the lower slopes of Mount Kilimanjaro, in Tanzania, that cater guided climbs to the mountain's summit. And I've had a thing for Kilimanjaro since catching a glimpse of the summit while on safari in Tanzania several years before. To real mountaineers, Kilimanjaro is a sissy mountain. Although the summit is the highest point on the continent of Africa, its elevation above sea level is a mere 19,340 feet. The climb is said to be strenuous, but non-technical. The travel industry advertises it like it's a walk in the park. A luxury safari. Perfect. After all, I didn't need a seminal mountaineering experience, just an eclectic adventure.

The most popular route to the summit is via the Marangu Route, quaintly referred to in guidebooks as the "Tourist Route". The guidebooks say the summit can be reached in three or four days, by a "reasonably fit" person. Porters carry the gear and cook the food, and it only costs about US$600. After hastily dismissing the relevance of age (I was then fifty-two), and after some very delicate negotiations with my wife (using the tired argument that it's cheaper than staying home), I called my friend John, a British ex-pat living in Nairobi, Kenya, chatted him up on the idea, and we decided to go for it.

Although there are scores of mountains in the world taller than Kilimanjaro, there are few so regal. Kilimanjaro is massive at its base, measuring roughly thirty-eight miles long, by twenty-four miles wide. It was born of three distinct volcanoes: Shira, whose highest point is 13,650 feet; Mawenzi, with a sharp Alpine spike at 16,896 feet; and Kibo, whose highest point is 19,340 feet. Kibo is topped by a large conical crater, thought to be dormant. The highest point along the circular rim of the crater is called Uhuru Peak, and that is Kilimanjaro's true summit. All together, Mount Kilimanjaro is a staggering assemblage of topography. And it is the anchor tenant of the vast land below.

When fickle heavens deign to part the hazy clouds obscuring the summit, a broad, convex silhouette appears, glistening white with snow and glacial ice. Down the gradually sloping mountainside, the brightness fades to the grey sheen of naked Mother Earth. Farther down, past the fertile farms and coffee plantations that dot the hillside, the gentle slope continues, a long long way, as if there is no end, to dusty plains and languid villages. There, in the mountain's glorious shadow, imperious giraffe glide to lunch on thorny acacia trees beside dry river beds, and big cats take down antelope, as routinely as we buy bread, while angry buzzards circle relentlessly overhead, in anticipation of the spoils. Herds of elephant, zebra, wildebeest, antelope and cape buffalo, share lean water holes without declaring war; and tiny brown huts, built of mud, dung and urine, baked hard by the hot sun, house the stately

Maasai, and their newborn cattle, and swarms of black flies. All in exquisite harmony.

At John's house in Nairobi, in mid-January, we assembled our climbing party, all first-timers: John, 42; John's two sons, Ben, 18, and Zack, 14; John's friend, a colorful chap named Paul, also 42; and me.

We were, if nothing else, eager souls. John has run a few marathons, and exercises regularly at his club. Ben practices Tae Kwon Do and is on the track team in college. Zack, although slightly built, is active in a variety of sports at school, and bristles with the vigor of youth. Paul, an American ex-pat living in Nairobi, was a distance runner in college, exercises only moderately, smokes cigarettes, and exudes enthusiasm. I was a half-ass athlete in college, so long ago it is of no consequence for purposes of fitness, but maybe for confidence. In my dotage, I do a little skiing, run a few miles each day, and indulge my fantasies with the occasional 10K. I call it a Titanic Struggle with Father Time. My wife calls it a Peter Pan Complex.

We held the obligatory testosterone conference and unanimously agreed that we were all "reasonably fit." What went unsaid, but hung in the air like a low cloud, was a challenge, each to the others, to prevail in this adventure. Such is the male curse.

We set out from Nairobi in John's four-wheel-drive Mitsubishi Pajero, to the jumping-off point, the Marangu Hotel in Tanzania, situated at elevation 4,500 feet, on the southern slopes of Kilimanjaro.

Departure from Nairobi. Paul, Ben, John, Zack and the author.

Once a farm, the Marangu Hotel has made a graceful transition to tourism, and now specializes in catering Kilimanjaro climbs. The hotel entrance driveway leads to a colorfully landscaped courtyard that was originally the barnyard. A small, one-room reception, and a closet-size gift shop, bracket the courtyard. Adjacent to the courtyard, in a dining room cleverly converted from the stables, four-place tables are primly set with white tablecloths and flower centerpieces. White-coated waiters hustle cheerfully to and fro from a kitchen located sadistically far from the dining room.

Guests are comfortably accommodated in rustic, one-story, duplex bungalows, scattered randomly about a neatly manicured hillside. Squeaky-clean guest rooms, accessed with prison-size door keys, are appointed with rickety steel-frame twin beds, early-campground furniture, threadbare cotton carpets on hardwood floors, and cast-iron bath-tubs. There is plenty of solar-heated hot water. The electricity comes on at 6:00 PM, because it isn't needed until then.

A centrally located bungalow is the bar. It is stocked with cold Tusker beer and soft drinks, and the service is superbly unsullied by Western notions of "fast food."

Bougainvillea, Birds of Paradise and esoteric flowering plants hug the walkways and buildings, while Guinea Fowls dart frantically about, begging to be drop-kicked into the Dik Dik pen. Somewhere there is a pool. Banana and coffee farms dominate the neighborhood, while clouds skirt the top of Kilimanjaro many miles distant and 15,000 feet above.

Service personnel, from the region's indigenous Wachagga tribe, are numerous, courteous, helpful and friendly.

The guidebooks shamelessly give the Marangu Hotel three-stars. I disagree. A day here outshines a week at Pebble Beach.

After dinner, the hotel's proprietor, Seamus (pronounced: "SHAY-miss"), summoned us to a half-hour pre-climb briefing. We attended reluctantly, somewhat annoyed to be lectured like schoolchildren, on the subject of hiking up a hill, by a pasty-white Caucasian, who more closely resembled a concert pianist than a mountain man. We were judging a book by its cover; and not for the first time would we feel like fools. Seamus was born of British parents, grew up in Tanzania, and has hiked to the summit several times.

In a subtle guise of dispensing helpful pointers for easy summiting, Seamus began to describe a program for staying alive.

"Whoa, whoa? What the f-f-f-f-f-f-f...?"

Staying alive? Jesus Christ. Aren't we just hiking up a hill? Seamus 1; All-Boys 0.

Like a seasoned actor working the audience, Seamus described the Wachagga term "pole pole" (pronounced as one word: "POH-lay-POH-lay"), which means "go slowly." A too rapid gain in altitude can scramble one's system like eggs in a fry-pan, he explained, therefore the practice of "pole pole" is crucial to longevity.

"There is no reward for being first to the top," Seamus grinned, enjoying the discomfort on our faces, "only for getting there."

Seamus was just getting warmed up. Most climbers, he explained, will experience Acute Mountain Sickness, or AMS: varying degrees of headache, nausea, loss of appetite, vomiting, exhaustion, insomnia, rapid pulse rate even at rest, swelling of the hands or face, and reduced urine output. AMS is the most common altitude-inspired affliction, and can be mitigated by drinking copious quantities of water and by taking the drug Diamox. A less common—but potentially fatal—affliction is Oedema, which is caused by an excessive accumulation of serous fluid in bodily tissues. Oedema comes in two flavors: Pulmonary and Cerebral. Pulmonary Oedema is characterized by the thrill of AMS plus gurgling sounds in the lungs, blood-tinged sputum, cold clammy skin, and bluish lips. Cerebral Oedema is characterized by severe headache, lack of coordination, and hallucination. The only treatment for either Oedema is immediate descent. Seamus' ability to command the attention of his audience took on mythic proportions.

On a roll, Seamus trickled out nuggets of additional life-preserving information: drink a minimum of three liters of liquids a day, eat regularly, get as much sleep as possible, wear sunglasses, and use sun block against the high-altitude UV rays. And for every step of the climb, use a walking stick, which he provided as a routine courtesy, in recognition of the fact that a long wood pole is not a common accouterment of the gentleman traveler.

Seamus concluded with special advice regarding wardrobe for the final ascent to the summit: three layers of pants, five layers of tops, two layers of gloves, ski goggles and a wool hat or balaclava over the ears. "Lastly," he said with an impish grin, "as you near the summit, put your drinking flasks and cameras inside your jackets to keep 'em from freezing."

So you could say we swallowed our pride; or you could say we attained enlightenment; or you could say we ascended from Dumb-fucksville. And to all you would be correct.

I slept well that night, properly humbled, ready for tomorrow, and blissfully unaware of the *other* importance of tomorrow: it was the day we would meet Moris.

Moris. Chief Guide. The Man.

Day 1

✦

Park Headquarters to Mandara Hut

WE ROSE EARLY and met our guides and porters, who stood in a row in the courtyard. Our party of five was assigned three guides and ten porters, all Wachagga gentlemen, tall and lean, without an ounce of body fat. Our Chief Guide, Moris, age 64, a book that *could be* judged by its cover, wore a friendly smile on a weathered bronze face that has seen the summit hundreds of times. That's his job. He gets $24 a day. Moris's son, Simoni, also a guide, was second in command. Simoni spoke English sparingly, but in sentences, whereas his father knew only four English words (or maybe *used* only four English words). The third guide, whose name sounded like "Dismos", was also the chief cook, and, thankfully, spoke some English. The porters, who get $12 a day for carrying mountains of gear and food on their heads to the last bivouac point, Kibo Hut, at elevation 15,500 feet, milled about looking refreshingly cheerful considering the nature of the work that would earn them that pay.

Seamus' people ferried us a few kilometers up the mountain in a rickety truck to the Marangu trailhead, located at the Park Headquarters of Kilimanjaro National Park, elevation 6,000 feet. There, they arranged our permit and sent us on our way at about 11:00 AM.

Not ten steps into the trail, we were, met with a trio of signs, designed to corroborate the advice of a pre-climb briefing, or in the absence of one, to provide a proper disclaimer. I spent a few minutes perusing these signs, appreciating the opportunity to put away any last-minute second guesses.

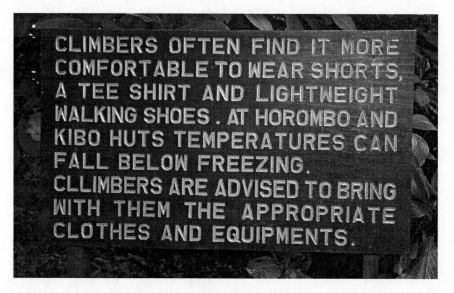

First sign.

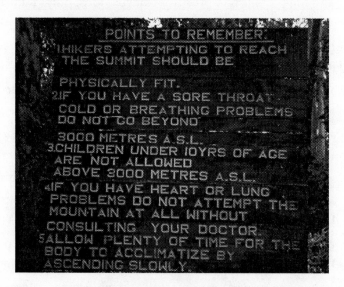

Second sign. 3000 metres = 9843 feet.

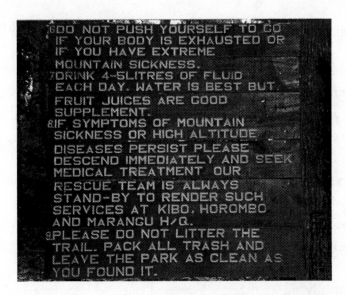

Third sign.

At last, we were off. We would traverse five distinct climate zones: 1. Cultivated Lower Slope; 2. Rain Forest; 3. Heath & Moorland; 4. High Desert; and 5. Summit. We would overnight at three locations while ascending approximately 13,340 feet to the summit, Uhuru Peak, elevation 19,340 feet. The round trip would take six days, four up and two down. We would cover a total distance of approximately 100 kilometers, about 65 miles. The Tourist Route.

We were all quite fashionably attired that first day, in clean shorts, dry tee shirts, sunglasses, day-pack with our lunch, and SPF 50 sunblock slathered all over. The weather was balmy and we were giddy as schoolchildren. The first part of the trail was an old vehicle track, rutted and pock-marked as if shelled by mortar fire. We started slow and tentative, in appreciation of Seamus' graphic briefing. The porters, on the other hand, took off like a shot, with massive burdens perched on their heads as comfortably as we carry change in our pockets. Moris shadowed us like a mother tending a child's first step. Years of experience had taught him to stay close to the *Mazungus* until he had their measure.

Inside of an hour we passed out of the Cultivation zone and into the Rain Forest. By now it was steamy-hot and we were sweating profusely; but we were too ecstatic from the juncture of adventure and danger to be uncomfortable. We laughed, told jokes, stopped to pee, and unanimously agreed that Life Was Great…and that we were cool.

Climbers in various stages of disarray passed us coming down. Those who had reached the summit were proud to say so if you asked. They had a glow. A greater proportion had not, and those you could spot, because they looked like dogs had played with them under a house.

Eventually the vehicle track petered out and became a rocky trail, steeper but easy to follow. A blazing sun stole through the trees forcing us to prefer the shady parts of the trail. Black and white Colobus Monkeys darted crazily through treetops filled with chattering birds. Gradually our initial jitters faded. We settled into an easy pace…and became Team Pole Pole. Abruptly, I was visited by a warm calm, as if a great weight had been lifted from my shoulders; and I was reminded—to draw a military analogy—of the significance of knowing when to attack and when to withdraw. At this particular *moment*, here in mighty Africa, my business world *had no moment*, and the tiniest bits of it could not be dredged from my memory by any force of nature. And that was a *very* good thing.

After four and a half hours, the trail opened onto a lush clearing, a gentle grassy slope dotted with small A-frame wood cabins. Solar panels located on the roofs of the cabins energized storage batteries for night lights. A larger A-frame was a "dining hall", with a second-story sleeping dormitory, and dominated the center of the clearing. Two squatter-style outhouses teetered at the perimeter of the clearing. Our porters lounged in the grass smoking black jagged roots. They had been there for an hour. Mandara Hut, elevation 8,856 feet.

Mandara Hut. Porters lounging.

We packed into our cabin and flopped down to relax. Almost immediately Moris appeared with hot tea, and rattled off something in an incomprehensible tongue which we took for Wachagga. Without translation, we knew immediately that he was saying: "You will stay alive if you drink this stuff when I offer it." The use of English to convey this message was superfluous.

I began to develop an affection for Moris, not merely because his tutelage was crucial to my longevity, but because his spirit was uncluttered and free. He was totally indifferent to language barriers, and regularly commenced conversation in Wachagga, as if it was our mother tongue as well. Eventually, I caught on, and thereafter responded cordially in English and some Swahili I had picked up in Kenya. Very often in these conversations, as with the tea admonition, I understood him perfectly. I got the impression, from the twinkling of his deep-set eyes, that he understood me as well.

As if the four-and-a-half-hour hike were insufficient exercise for one day, Ben and Zach sought more. They fashioned a football out of a roll of toilet paper and duct tape and took turns going deep. I admired the youthful enthusiasm that *they* took for granted, but that had slipped past *me* one day when I wasn't looking. As further remonstrance on the subject of lost youth, I prayed they wouldn't render the toilet paper useless for its intended purpose.

At dinnertime Moris fetched us from our hut and shepherded us to the "dining hall," like kids at summer camp, where our porters had set places for us at long wood tables. We sat cheek-by-jowl with other climbers, whose places had been set by their porters, and were served our dinner. It seemed quite absurd. The All-Boys Perilous African Adventure.

We were first served "soup", a loose term for a dish that was some-times flavored water, sometimes lumpy porridge, and was always tasty, regardless of its composition. Unlike the tea, it would not become repugnant with altitude. A main course of meat and vegetables, and a dessert of papaya, were traveling well at this early stage of the trip. They would not always.

The one-room, A-frame sleeping huts accommodated only four per-sons; and since there were five in our party, Paul gracefully volunteered to take the first turn in another hut with two strangers, Hans and Franz, brothers, the Austrian National Snoring Champions. That night, Paul was reminded graphically that no act of good will goes unpunished.

Of course, Hans and Franz were not their real names. To learn the real names of fellow travelers would dissolve their caricature and diminish my adventure; consequently I went to great lengths to avoid learning any true identities, and indulged my own brand of perverse pleasure in assigning names that simply ought to be.

Day 2

◆

Mandara Hut to Horombo Hut

SIMONI WOKE US at 6:30 AM, with a thermos of hot tea, and a hub-cap full of hot water for all of us to wash in. Nobody wanted to be first with the tea, nor last with the water.

We dressed more warmly for this day's hike. Paul broke out a pair long pants, painfully hot-pink in color, and donned them with a flourish. His golf pants. He said he loves them. He bought them on sale somewhere for US$12, proving that, to a chosen few, cost is no object.

The trail out of Mandara Hut, at first steep and moist, wound over exposed roots and jutting rocks made slick from the morning dew. After half an hour, we emerged almost instantly from the rain forest onto alpine meadow, the third climate zone, Heath and Moorland, dotted with heather, protea, and other scrubby heath-like vegetation. The sky was immaculately clear. Kibo and Mawenzi Peaks shimmered in the morning sun high above us. Mawenzi's jagged peaks, on our right, contrasted with the gentle expanse of Kibo, our destination, dead ahead and a long way off. We were less than halfway to the summit, and already my feet were complaining, and my thighs were burning. A test of will was imminent.

Higher up, and hours later, Heath gave way to the Moorland, dotted with giant Scenecios and Lobelias, high desert succulents. The Scenecios, cactus trees with one or two fat branches topped with a rosette of leaves, growing to a height of thirty feet, mixed like Mutt and

Jeff with the Lobelias, single, meter-high phallic stalks, with sharp downward thrusting scales along the sides, and a spray of long thin leaves circling the base. I thought of Sesame Street.

Above 12,000 feet, I began to experience shortness of breath and the term "pole pole" began to earn its reputation. The trail wound over myriad rocks and boulders defining broad hillocks, through wide ravines bisected by trickling streams, and through muddy bogs…inexorably *up*.

At some point, the front of Paul's left boot separated from the sole and flapped open like an old dog's mouth. Paul had purchased these hiking boots on sale, three days ago, in Dubai. He had found yet another bargain, proving that he should not be allowed to shop alone. He lashed the sole to the rest of the boot with twine from the end of my walking stick and we continued on.

About 3:00 PM, we lumbered into Horombo Hut, at 12,340 feet. We had covered about ten miles in six hours, and had gained over 3,300 feet of altitude. My legs were rubbery, and it was time for Advil. We flopped down in our hut to rest, and Simoni magically appeared with hot tea. I wolfed down my share, despite the unsettling observation that it was beginning to taste like sterno.

Horombo Hut. Kibo summit ever visible above left.

Horombo Hut looks like Mandara Hut with the rain forest napalmed away. The sleeping huts and the "dining hall" are identical to Mandara Hut's. A dull afternoon haze created the illusion of a nineteenth-century, High Sierra mining camp.

But unlike Mandara Hut, the squatters are located in the middle of the camp, which is a curious location for sanitary facilities with a life of their own. Squatter No. 1, we soon learned, was given to flushing upwards, randomly and for no apparent reason, sending rivulets of water (and other stuff) sleuthing through the camp between the huts. This phenomenon is attributable to the vicissitudes of the gentle but erratic mountain creek above the camp that flushes the squatters naturally via an underground stream. This phenomenon also begs a simple question of fluid mechanics: if a fierce rainstorm turns the gentle creek into a raging torrent, won't Squatter No. 1 resemble Old Faithful? The answer was provided at Paul's expense that very day, as if a higher power had found a perfect parallel for mischief. Blissfully unaware that it had commenced to rain heavily above the camp, Paul made his daily pilgrimage to a squatter, and randomly chose No. 1. While Paul was deep in squat, and deeper still in abstract thought, Old Faithful let loose, ejecting Paul from the squatter at light speed, bouncing and flapping, as would a duck with its ass on fire.

Before leaving the subject of Squatter No. 1, I am compelled to pause for a moment and consider the question of why the squatters are numbered in the first place. There were, you see, a No. 2 and a No. 3. To what purpose, the numbering? Are we to schedule meetings with our comrades at one or the other, and therefore need to know which is which? Are reservations for a specific squatter taken by camp staff? Or is it simply that Paul's experience is a theatrical event, designed by a crafty promoter, who charges a fee for the show and employs a number system to identify the venue?

By now, it should be apparent to the reader that the effects of altitude start early, are unpredictable, and are not all bad. And as if these observations were not apparent to the five of us, an example presented itself just before dinner; Johnnie showed up to introduce himself.

"Hi, I'm Johnnie," he bellowed absently, pronouncing it like "Joanie." "I'm the Rescue Captain."

His movements were agitated like a coke addict, but his demeanor was friendly like a car salesman. He wore the vacuous smile of a crash-test dummy, and his eyes were bugged out and glassy. I was enthralled. Was this the stuff of legends, a true mountain madman? But no. Johnnie's breath revealed the mundane truth; he was just plastered. This was a rare glimpse of the mixture of grain alcohol and altitude. To Johnnie's credit, however, and in spite of *his* condition, he had come to check on *our* condition, and to inform us that he was the Rescue Captain…and that he was *on duty*.

"You gotta be shittin' me." I turned to John, "he's shittin' me, right?"

John was speechless; his eyes were wide as saucers, and his mouth was frozen open in a rictus of amazement. We looked at each other. Had we heard correctly? The Rescue Captain? On duty? Are we both hallucinating? Is it AMS? Cerebral Oedema?

Or maybe Johnnie's onto something, an ingenious tactic: above 12,000 feet, he scrambles his brain with low-grade hooch, then breathes on the *Mazungus* and tells them he's the *on-duty* Rescue Captain. This focuses them so pointedly on safety that he doesn't have to rescue them. *Voila!*

Rescue Captain? Author with Johnnie.

It worked on me. I silently pledged to stay safe in order to avoid Johnnie's services. Logically, this episode led me to consider personal hygiene as a crucial component of safety, so I set about my daily *toi-lette*. And because there are no bathing facilities on the mountain, and also because the creek water was too frigid to bear, I got the bright idea to improvise with a pile of Handi-Wipes that I had purloined from Lufthansa Airlines. I soon made two discoveries, which I shall pass on to fellow travelers: 1. Handi-Wipes are indeed handy, hence the name;

and 2. Handi-Wipes that contain alcohol are eminently unsuitable for cleansing one's genitals.

Day 3

✦

Rest Day at Horombo Hut

NO HIKING TODAY. We napped mostly, to acclimate to the altitude, and to rest in preparation for the remainder of the climb. It's a good thing for me that we did, because it turned out to be a day of serious bowel insubordination.

Most every lily-white tourist (such as yours truly), who ventures adventurously into the Third World, will experience some flavor of bowel insubordination there. It is ordained.

The first hint of it is a short pulse received by an unsuspecting brain, a message in the form of a mild spike that is processed and understood in a nano-second. It is a singularly awful feeling. A feeling one would trade for a root canal. In another nano-second, as forceful and unstoppable as the tides of Nova Scotia, comes rumbling in the bowels, beads of sweat on the brow, interruption of social discourse in mid-sentence, fear of impending embarrassment, abandonment of such fear, and a reckless dash to the can. The shits. There are more delicate terms, but none better.

Such was my fate on this otherwise fine day, exactly as described. The vagaries of Wachagga food preparation engaged my intestinal tract in full fury. I hit the squatters on a dead run, caring not which number to avoid, and emptied my soul. "Ahhhhh!"

How clever and efficient I had thought our porters were, when earlier I had seen them scrubbing the cooking pots with the same rags

14

they wound in a circle and wore on their sweaty heads to steady their heavy loads.

The only constructive enterprise of the day was the repair of Paul's boots. Hiking boots of minimal utility, decades old, and worn to a frazzle by a thousand hikers, were available for rental at Horombo Hut. Fighting a natural propensity, Paul wisely decided not to avail himself of this dubious commercial enterprise. Utilizing duct tape and super glue, a Rube Goldberg repair was effected and Paul's Dubai Specials were placed back in service.

Day 4

◆

Horombo Hut to Kibo Hut

PROMPTLY AT 7:00 AM, Simoni woke us with his hubcap of water and thermos of hot tea. Altitude was having its way with my taste buds and I could no longer abide the demon tea. Nor could I abide the water I had been mixing with Gatorade powder to mask the bitter taste caused by purification tablets. This artifice had worked until about 12,000 feet, at which altitude the mixture began to taste like sewer water. Eventually, I learned that normal hikers utilize a simple pump, with a purifying filter, to produce clean tasty drinking water. I had out-smarted myself again.

We said goodbye to Johnnie. He was loaded again, or perhaps still loaded, we couldn't tell which. The difference was academic. Then I noticed Johnnie's rescue vehicle, waiting under a hut for its call to action. It was vintage Dr. Suess: a unicycle, with a steel-framed stretcher mounted horizontally in place of the seat. There were bicycle-type handlebars at each end of the stretcher for the rescuers to guide the thing. The rear handlebars had handbrakes…which would be oper-ated by…whom…presumably…the Rescue Captain? By Johnnie? Somewhere in the ozone between imagination and hallucination, I could see Johnnie trundling some poor sonofabitch down the hill on this contraption…with the White Rabbit guiding the front end.

As I was struggling back to reality, Paul hauled out a day-glow-orange Kalamazoo College sweatshirt and put it on over his hot-pink pants.

Trail to Kibo Hut. Kibo summit in background above left.

A couple of hours later, just above 13,000 feet, moving slowly and breathlessly in the warm morning sun, we passed into the fourth climate zone, the High Desert, where water is scarce, UV radiation intense, and temperatures extreme. Here, sturdy desert flowers emerge miraculously from inhospitable soil, disrupted continually by frost and ice.

At about 13,500 feet, we crossed a tiny mud hole, where a small plastic pipe dribbled cold water, and a sign that required no elaboration read "Last Water Point."

Last Water. Last chance.

The pitch of the trail eased mercifully, as we entered the Saddle, a barren bowl-shaped wasteland, connecting Kibo and Mawenzi Peaks. Husbanding energy, we trudged silently across a veritable moonscape of strewn boulders and volcanic gravel, coughed up by eruption aeons ago. Here, the hardiest flowering plants gave way to green moss balls and dull red lichens that prefer lava rocks and boulders to the moving soil.

The air became ever thinner, our pace became ever slower, and our gait ever ponderous. At some vague point, Kibo Hut became visible as a dark speck, far off in the distance. It appeared deceptively close, although we would not reach it for several more hours. I thought I saw a mirage. I thought of AMS. Then a soft headache developed, and I thought of Cerebral Oedema. These thoughts were doing me no good at all, so I thought about the Counting Crows, bellowed "Mister Jones", and plodded on.

About 3:30 PM, we inched into Kibo Hut, now nestled in cloud cover, at elevation 15,520 feet. We had been hiking for six and a half hours, but it felt like ten.

Kibo Hut consists of four dreary stone buildings, the largest and most prominent of which is the *Mazungus'* barracks, divided into five sleeping rooms, each containing six double-decker bunk beds. There is a small barracks for guides and porters, and two tiny cook shacks. Fifty yards downhill from the barracks, a filthy stone outhouse—denied the attention of flies, courtesy of the altitude—awaited the unlucky.

Kibo Hut. Cold and in the clouds.

The only fuel at this elevation, is carried on the heads of the porters, and since they carry enough only for cooking, there are no heaters or fireplaces anywhere. Warmth, like beauty, is in the eye of the beholder, and I found it in thermal underwear inside my sleeping bag.

We found our assigned room, and within ten minutes, Simoni was there with hot tea and biscuits. Constant Paul was the only one to touch the biscuits, and John the only one to take the tea. Zack somehow ascertained that there were Cokes for sale, and scored one for himself, and one for Ben. I drank plain water, purified by John's pump.

Huddled around a table that occupied too much of the room, sat Muriel and George, a diminutive British couple with porcelain skin and translucent hair, most assuredly septuagenarians. They sat across from each other trading vitriolic barbs that proved they had been married since the Ice Age. They were tattered and drawn, and looked like they would stroke out just weeding a garden, but somehow they had beat us to Kibo Hut.

Our other roommates were: Biff and Shank, two aristocratic Aryans, blonds, twenty-ish, Malibu surfer-types; Abu Fluffy, an overtly fashionable terrorist-look-alike, of indeterminate sex and ethnicity, mute rather than unfriendly; and, guess who, the snorers, Hans and Franz. Altogether, a full count of twelve in our room for the night.

Dinner was served about 5:00 PM. The "soup" was still tasty, but it was thicker than usual, owing either to the altitude or to something I didn't want to think about. Someone enjoyed pointing out that the "soup" was sticking to my chin, instead of dripping off like it usually did, but I wasn't aware of it. The main course consisted of the little round roasted potatoes that traveled well, and something Simoni said was meat that didn't. John, Ben and Zack picked at their food without interest, while Paul ate like a condemned man at his last meal. I couldn't get beyond the soup, and I was getting nauseous just watching Paul. Then Simoni delivered a pulsating culture that was once a papaya and I ran from the room.

By now, the altitude was affecting everyone, but in varying degrees. My headache had gotten worse, and John and Ben had one too. I began to get paranoid about Cerebral Oedema. I remembered Seamus' explanation, that a simple AMS headache can be mitigated by aspirin or pain killer, whereas Cerebral Oedema is totally unaffected by medication, and can be relieved only by immediate descent. I bet the ranch on AMS, took two more Advil, and passed the bottle around.

By 6:00 PM, everyone was in their sleeping bags for the night. Sleep was illusive, however, thanks to AMS and the melodies supplied by the Austrian National Snoring Champions. But I must have gotten a few winks because I dreamt that someone was drilling through the wall.

Day 5

◆

Kibo Hut to Uhuru Peak
and
Uhuru Peak to Horombo Hut

LIGHTS CAME ON at midnight, and a day one never forgets began. Suddenly, the room was alive with guides waking their charges. I came out of a fitful sleep, and my first cognizant thought was of howling wind. That's because the wind was howling. It was, I would soon learn, also freezing-ass cold. Simoni appeared, cheerfully waving a thermos of hot tea, and badgered me out of my sleeping bag. I wanted to kill him. The room resounded with whining complaints of headache and fatigue. Everyone was up, except Hans the Younger, who had a crippling case of AMS, and wisely elected to stay in bed. I envied him. The count of those in our room going for the summit was now eleven of twelve.

The place was electric with tension, as everyone scrambled into the day's uniform. I felt light-headed. The exercise of dressing required great thought, even though I had rehearsed it in my mind, everyday for the past week. A first layer of thermal underwear, which, like everyone else, I had slept in, then a tee shirt, a long-sleeve jersey, a wool sweater, jeans, shell-pants, gators, ski jacket, scarf, skiing goggles, mittens and wool hat. Around the room, I saw that everyone looked a little different, yet they all looked the same.

Eight or ten climbing parties, including ours, assembled outside under a cold half moon. In spite of our diminished faculties, the five of us were so intense that we functioned with the efficiency of a well-trained military unit. We checked our own gear, checked each others' gear, cinched up our packs, and formed up single-file behind our commander, Moris the Great. Simoni and Dismos were there too, making eight in our party for the final ascent.

Starting from Kibo Hut at elevation 15,520 feet, we would make for Uhuru Peak at 19,340 feet. I hadn't thought to do the math before, but I did it now: 3,820 feet of altitude gain in about seven hours. Holy shit! Apprehension and serenity mixed in my head illogically. I never felt more alive.

We pushed off at 1:15 AM, in the middle of a slow parade of climbing parties. The first leg of the day's climb, to Gilman's Point at 18,635 feet, where the mountainside meets the crater rim, would take five hours. According to my crude (after-the-fact) calculation, the average slope from Kibo Hut to Gilman's Point is in excess of 27 percent. This grade would be the steepest of the entire climb.

The trail was principally scree, loose volcanic gravel, ranging in size from small stones to powder. In the light of the wan moon, the trail was discernable only to Moris, unlike the trail of earlier days that was so obvious we often skipped along like Dorothy and Toto on the Yellow Brick Road. I offered Moris the goofy-looking miner's headlamp I had brought as an extra precaution, and surprisingly, he accepted it. After hundreds of these ascents, he was taking no chances.

As we went higher, the trail got steeper. Footing became more tenuous, as we fought the infamous mountain scree that dogs every step. Step forward, slide backwards. I cursed the scree. The trail soon became switchbacks, too steep for direct ascent. And as we got clumsier, Moris got smoother. His hiking rhythm, unchanged since the first day, was a study of grace and efficiency. His stride was to the mountain, as a camel's is to the desert. I had tried, on several occasions, to duplicate Moris' stride, but could not accomplish, in a few days, what he had perfected in a lifetime. No one could.

As we continued on, breathing became more difficult. My heart rate was increasing steadily from the exertion, acerbated by the oxygen deprivation. It was getting steadily colder, and I began to feel it in my fingertips. We stopped frequently, leaned on our hiking sticks and gulped for air. We dared not sit down, because getting back up is too tiring, and sitting too long can cause a chill. At every rest-stop I drank from the water bottle secreted inside my jacket, and silently thanked Seamus for the tip.

Sometimes, parties passed us on the trail, sometimes we passed them. Sequence was not important, nor was time, only breathing and "pole pole." The effects of altitude gain, different from person to person, and not necessarily a function of fitness, were becoming more acute. John told of a strange theory, related to him by veteran mountain guides, to the effect that smokers, whose systems are accustomed to oxygen deprivation, do not suffer the effects of altitude gain as seriously as non-smokers. Sounded like bullshit to me. But perhaps we were seeing it. Paul, the smoker, always took the point, ahead of the rest of us, none of whom have never smoked a cigarette. Paul would be the first in our party to reach the summit; and he would do so without great breathing difficulty. Go figure.

More than halfway to Gilman's Point, moving slower, but steadily up the loose scree, it got even colder. Although my feet were warm inside two layers of socks, and my ears were comfortable under a wool ski hat, my fingers were freezing inside my ski mittens. Paul complained that his hands were warm, but his toes were cold inside his Dubai Specials. We were all feeling the cold, which required more frequent rest stops. My spirit began to morph, from determination to anger, directed at the insidious scree, that slipped and slid beneath every step. Step and slide, step and slide. Slide just a little…but with every step. Then I began to muse philosophical. Was I merely *looking* at the scree? Was I *looking*, and not *seeing*? Was I insensitive to our intrusion on the immaculate mountain? Was I not *seeing* the scree as one of Nature's sublime defensive measures, like the white coat of a polar bear or the harsh truth of a drought? Clearly not. I would have liked to reflect on this observation a while longer, but hallucination was not out of the question, and, besides, I was freezing my ass off.

Gilman's Point became visible, from time to time, high above, in the semi-darkness, but its proximity, like the proximity of Kibo Hut the day before, was an illusion. We paused in the lee of some boulders, and I sat down this time because I was exhausted. As I sat, gobbling candy and gasping for air, I noticed Simoni scramble over to John.

"Trouble, Bwana, come," said Simoni.

He led John up the scree, a few yards, to where Zack was sprawled out on his back, in the wind, out of cover, breathing heavily, sweating, shivering and starting to chill. At fourteen, perhaps too young for his system to withstand this kind of assault, Zack had been fooled by the illusion that Gilman's Point was only a few yards away. Apparently, he had broken away from the switchback path, and had charged straight up the scree. Dutifully, Simoni had stayed with him, but Zack had flamed out, and flopped down on his back. Now he was struggling with conflicting emotions. He knew he was finished, but he didn't want to be a quitter. He could not feel pride in the accomplishment of climbing to 17,000 feet, under his own steam, at fourteen. Perhaps that would come later. For now, Zack was feeling embarrassment and defeat. John was struggling with a difficult decision, for which he really had no choice. He understood that time was an enemy at this altitude and temperature. In Zack's emotional state, he would chill before he could recover. Moreover, there would be an additional risk of chill to the rest of us if we delayed any longer. Reluctantly, but correctly, John sent his son back down to Kibo Hut with Simoni. There were six us now, and we continued on. "Pole pole" is a harsh taskmaster, that strikes quickly when taken lightly.

At some point, a few hundred yards below Gilman's Point, the grade became even steeper and the trail less discernable. Nearing 6:00 AM, as the dawn sky lightened, I realized that the trail had faded away, and I was no longer bipedal. Nor was anyone else. We were scrambling on all fours, over rocks and boulders, simian fashion. Moris was no longer following a distinct pathway, because there was none, rather he was leading us to the crater rim, by the shortest route he could find. I felt utterly exhausted. My heart was beating so fast, I thought it would leap out of my chest. I thought it must be the same for the others. I heard some muted grumbling, but nobody stopped. I seemed to be carried by the momentum of the others, as if a cosmic force was overpowering the laws of physics. "Goddamn," I thought (or hallucinated), "why is this so exhilarating?" "Is there an essence of something here?" And then my reverie was interrupted by shouts of triumph, as one by one, we clambered over a boulder the size of a Volkswagen, and stumbled into a clearing the size of a bathtub, ringed by a windbreak of smaller boulders, and littered with hikers' trash. Gilman's Point, elevation 18,345 feet.

Everyone collapsed in a heap, drank water, ate candy, and gulped for air…even Moris. I found a rock for back support, fell against it half-supine, and started talking to my heart, like a boy to his dog. "Slow down…please…atta boy, slooow dowwnnnn." And like a dog, it would not obey. John told me later, that my lips were blue, but he didn't say anything at the time, because he wasn't sure if he was hallucinating, or if the color just looked good on me. Thanks, John.

About 6:00 AM, a pale sun crested the horizon. I was still laying there, vaguely aware that a beautiful sunrise was unfolding, when I heard a disembodied voice say, "look at that, it's beautiful," and I made some smart-ass reply like "yeah, right." But the sunrise brought a spark of animation to the group, and with it, a collective sense that the summit was attainable.

Before I knew it, someone was agitating to go again.

"Can't sit too long," another disembodied voice said, "you'll get a chill."

"Chill, schmill," I shot back, "I think my friggin' heart's gonna pop."

But I had to get up, because I could see the summit now, Uhuru Peak, the highest point in Africa, just over there, around the other side of the crater rim, 705 feet higher, and a couple of miles away…calling me.

A new wave of enthusiasm enveloped the group, a second wind. Paul and Ben stood, and shouldered their packs. Moris did too. John struggled to his feet, and social pressure plucked me from my daze. I was up. I was going. But where was the propulsion coming from? From the same force I felt in the final push to Gilman's Point? From Teamwork? Testosterone? The cosmos again?

Moris led, Paul and Ben were next, then John and I, followed by Dismos. The way around the crater rim was an actual trail again, gradual not steep, mostly over snow pack, rocks, and volcanic gravel. We descended a short way through hard snow, then started back up again. Always up, it seemed. I mused again, as was now my wont, that I must be buoyed along simply because reaching the summit would be the end of *up*.

Ben and John, with author in background. Departing Gilman's Point.

Paul, Ben and Moris forged on ahead of John and I. Paul, the smoker, did not seem to feel the oxygen deprivation. Ben, four days shy of nineteen, was indefatigable, as he should be at that age. Moris was just Superman. I trailed along last, more like Dopey than Doc.

Within a half-mile of the summit, the trail became a gently-ascending promenade. Even so, oxygen deprivation slowed John and me all the more. We staggered past towering glaciers that sparkled in the morning sun, and begged to be photographed. I knew that Global Warming was killing these glaciers, and that this was an historic opportunity to record a chapter in their demise. This knowledge was rendered vague, befuddled, and almost beyond my grasp because I was so exhausted. I fumbled for my camera, tried to get an Ansel Adams shot, and clicked on something. Whatever it was, it would have to do.

Glacier at summit. Ansel Adams shot.

As John and I drew to within a quarter-mile of the summit, we saw Paul and Ben there, jumping around, celebrating, while Moris scratched his head in wonderment. My heart was beating like a jack-hammer, and it wanted to explode and be relieved of its burdensome task, but the image of the celebrants on Uhuru Peak drew me on.

The length of a football field now. John and I, in tandem, slowed even more. Then John recalled another of Seamus' suggestions, and we started counting steps and breaths: 100 steps, stop, lean on the hiking stick, count 20 breaths, resume the pattern; 100 steps, stop, lean on stick, 20 breaths, etc. After ten minutes, we were too exhausted and too breathless to continue that pace, so we slowed to 75 steps and 30 breaths. In that fashion, and an eternity later, totally spent, I fell in the dirt, on Uhuru Peak. It was 7:50 AM, two hours after we had left Gilman's Point, and six and a half hours after we had left Kibo Hut.

Author at summit. Crater to the right. Glacier in background left.

"Tourist Route, my ass!"

For five minutes, I lay sprawled in the dust against a comfortable rock, gasping for air, in a vain attempt to lower my pulse rate. The effort yielded minimal results. At an altitude where atmospheric density is half that at sea level, every gulp gets you only half a load. Remember that, ye hot-shot skiers.

In the periphery of my cognizance, I sensed a celebration underway, but I was powerless to participate. Paul and Ben were drinking congratulatory toasts from a flask of Southern Comfort that John had been schlepping up the mountain for four days. Even John and Moris were participating. Someone tendered me a hit, and I waved him off as if it were hot lead. Ixnay on the Comfortnay.

Eventually, I recovered, enough to stand upright and even dance a little jig. We all hugged each other, and took pictures behind the faded wooden sign that read: "You Have Reached The Uhuru Peak, The

Highest Point in Africa." I was blindly euphoric, and I leaned on the sign just as someone yelled, "don't touch the sign," and it fell to the ground in pieces. The sharp *crack* of it hitting the ground startled me, as if I'd been slapped by a nurse. I shivered, and was immediately wracked with emotion. Embarrassed, I turned my back to the group, and walked away some yards, to be alone on the roof of Africa. Facing west, marveling at the sea of impenetrable clouds that obscured a view of the Serengeti below, I savored a most precious private moment. My chest heaved involuntarily, and I trembled with tearless sobs, that I did not expect, and will never be able to explain. Some Macho Man.

I returned to the group, and we started back down. To this day, I rejoice at the very sound of the word *down*.

Below Gilman's Point, I was able to regard the steep and pitiless scree in the full light of day. Scree that tormented us for five hours on the way up, now belched clouds of dust in our haggered faces as we coughed and stumbled in descent. It became obvious why the final ascent of the mountain begins in darkness.

Back at Kibo Hut, we pulled Zack from his sleeping bag, changed out of our dust-caked clothes, and tallied up the score of how many from our room had made it to the summit. Zack said that Muriel and George made it as far as Gilman's Point. He said they came back through the room a few hours earlier. Muriel was abusing George unmercifully, for stopping halfway up the scree to change clothes, apparently blaming him for their inability to reach the summit. Biff and Shank no longer affected superiority, because they too had to give up at Gilman's Point, as did Abu Fluffy. But Franz the Elder had reached the summit, so the score was five of twelve.

We collected Zack, and headed back down the Saddle towards Horombo Hut. As we descended, a headache which I had endured since arriving at Kibo Hut began to dissipate. Our pace now, although slow, was decidedly faster than going up, thanks to gravity. My thighs began to burn from the use of different muscle groups, and I longed for the luxury of a soft pallet. As ever, Paul led the way at a furious pace, for which he paid a hefty price. The Mountain God, apparently interpreting Paul's homeward-bound enthusiasm as disrespect for the mountain, pitched Paul headlong into numerous full-scree face-plants, until he figured it out and eased off on his pace. The timing of this episode was perfect for the rest of us, it seemed, and our howling laughter did not ease off.

When finally we arrived at Horombo Hut, Johnnie was there to greet us, looking rheumy as ever.

"Sorry Johnnie, I didn't need you," I said. Truth be told, it was close.

I found our hut, and flopped down on a rock-hard pallet softer than goose down. It was 3:45 PM, the end of a fourteen and a half hour day. I was burnt toast. The only thing more ragged than me was Paul's left boot, which was strangely intact, although the duct tape was now confetti.

We ate dinner early, and voraciously, thanks to taste buds restored by the lower altitude. By 6:00 PM, all five of us were in a comatose sleep that lasted for twelve and a half hours.

Day 6

✦

Horombo Hut to Park Headquarters

IN THE MORNING we made the home run, stopping briefly at Mandara Hut for lunch, then continuing down through the rain forest towards Park Headquarters.

Just before the trail ended, a lady holding a small child emerged magically from the bushes in front of Moris. The child produced a clean shirt and handed it to him. He changed shirts and handed back the dirty one. Smiles of affection were exchanged, but no words were spoken. His daughter and grand-daughter had come to play out a custom so elegant and poignant that its true meaning did not hit me until I started to write about it. Moris had worn the same shirt, ragged sweatshirt, and torn denim pants for the full six days we were together. In another context, he would have been mistaken for homeless. But on this occasion, when he would lead his *Mazungus* safely back into Park Headquarters, in completion of a professional responsibility of staggering proportions, he would do so in a clean shirt. There, on a muddy path on the sunny slopes of Tanzania, at the end of an event of no particular consequence to Western civilization, a man of no formal education and little material wealth, gave a world-class lesson in personal dignity.

Blissfully oblivious, tattered and filthy, John, Ben, Paul and I swaggered into Park Headquarters like conquering heroes, and received

33

diplomas certifying that we had attained the summit. Like we did something special. And at the time, it felt better than when I got my law degree. Ironically, Moris was the only one who had done anything special.

Then he went home.

Epilogue

IN FEBRUARY, 1998, Zack climbed to Point Lenana, elevation 16,355, on Mt. Kenya, Africa's second tallest mountain. Although guidebooks recommend the use of ice axe and crampons, Zack used neither. There are higher points on Mt. Kenya actually, the twin peaks, Batian at 17,058 ft., and Nelion at 17,022 ft. These peaks are steep, inhospitable, rocky crags, and they are climbed only by the most technically-skilled maniac.

In February, 2000, another of John's sons, Sam, then 18, also made it to Point Lenana with a group from his school in South Africa.

In April, 2006, John's daughter, Emily, 18, reached Kilimanjaro's Uhuru Peak with a group from her school in South Africa.

The odd thing about this altitude-based hiking is the randomness with which the Mountain God determines who shall reach a given summit and who shall not. Attributes, such as fitness, size, muscle-mass, education, net worth, or beauty, are not determinative. And MG doesn't give a rip about gender, age, weight, ethnicity, citizenship, or religion. Indeed, in our story, Hanz the Younger was a fine specimen of Teutonic manhood, who didn't even make it out of bed at Kibo Hut. On the other hand, his brother, Franz the Elder (whom I suspect might actually have been a twin) made it to the summit. Muriel and George were mere wisps of living tissue who could have made it to the summit, but were foiled by their own devices. Biff and Shank were gorgeous white boys, and Abu Fluffy was doggedly determined, but MG was unmoved and limited their fate to Gilman's Point. Paul, an exuberant middle-age smoker, was the first to reach the summit, followed by teen-age Ben. John and I, both middle age and dragging ass, were last.

Now back to Emily: all 95 pounds of her made it to the summit with no adverse consequences.

In summary, we are left with the conclusion that no logic or pattern can be discerned to predict the outcome of altitude hiking. So I guess it all comes back to "reasonably fit." If you are, give it a go, and hope MG likes you.

978-0-595-41625-7
0-595-41625-X

LaVergne, TN USA
26 November 2010
206341LV00001B/87/A